The bunnies are hungry and want to dine.
Can you help them? Just cut on each line.

Super Kid flies into the sky.
Cut on the lines to see how high.

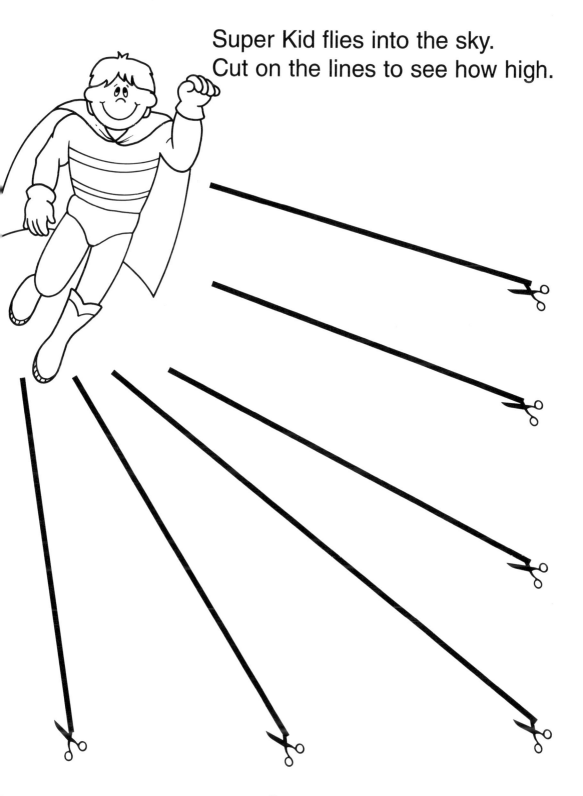

You can help these cute monkeys
To get a real treat.
Cut each line to a banana.
Do your best to be neat.

Each child shoots an arrow into the sky.
Cut it to make it reach a bull's-eye.

7

Each mouse is hungry for some cheese.
Cut on the lines, if you please.

These boys and girls are playing ball.
Cut on the lines so the
balls don't fall.

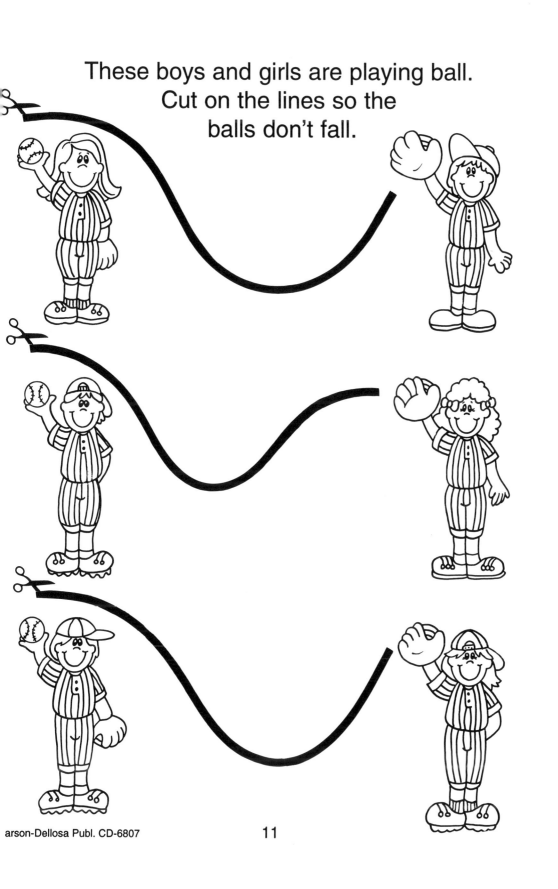

Each cat is hungry for a tasty dish.
Cut on the lines to reach the fish.

This shell is the house of Sally Snail.
Cut on the line to follow the trail.

Alley Gator's mixed up. His head's at his waist. You can fix him up with scissors and paste.

Cut out the pieces on the thick lines. Arrange correctly and paste on another sheet of paper.

Wilbur Walrus is missing his face.
Fix him with crayons, scissors and paste.

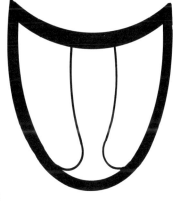

Print your name on the side of the submarine.

Cut on the thick lines and fold on the dotted line. The submarine will stand up.

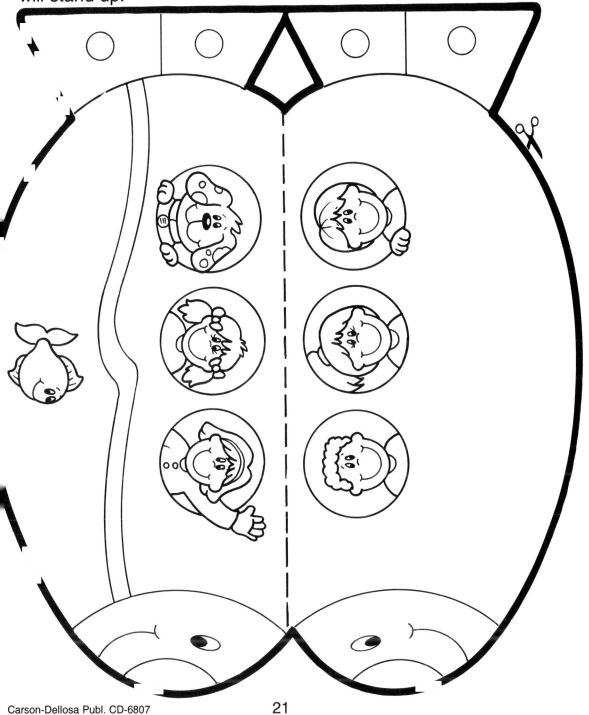

Swimming, camping, and hiking are fun.
Cut on the lines to make a sun.

If you put these pieces together
The way they should be,
You'll see a pot that is meant
To hold hot, tasty tea.

Cut on the thick lines. Arrange the pieces to make a teapot. Paste on
another sheet of paper. Color the picture.

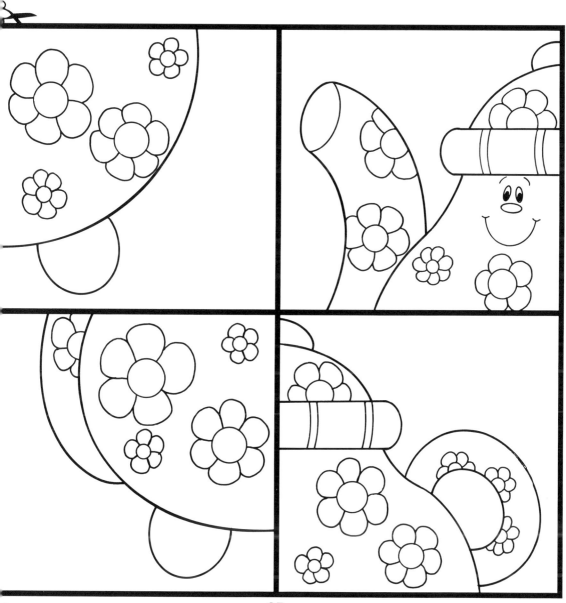

Color these flowers pretty and bright.
Then cut on the outside lines just right.

If you put each piece
In just the right place
You'll see Sammy's ready
To blast off in space.

Cut out the four pieces on the thick lines. Arrange correctly and paste on another sheet of paper. Color the picture.

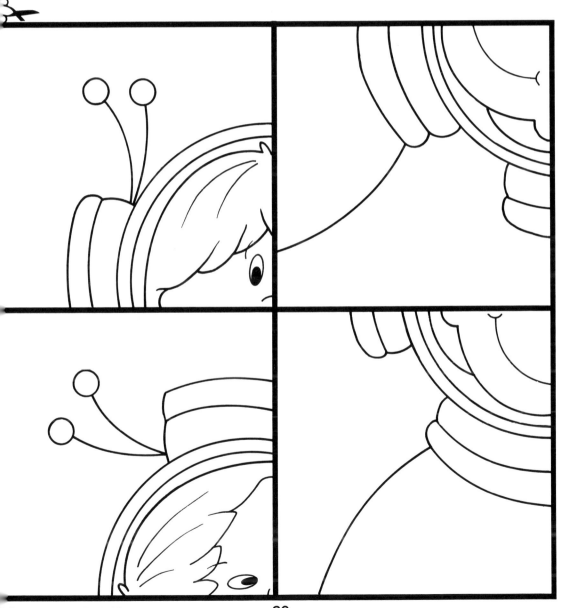

The turtle wants to
run a race.
Put each foot in
its proper place.

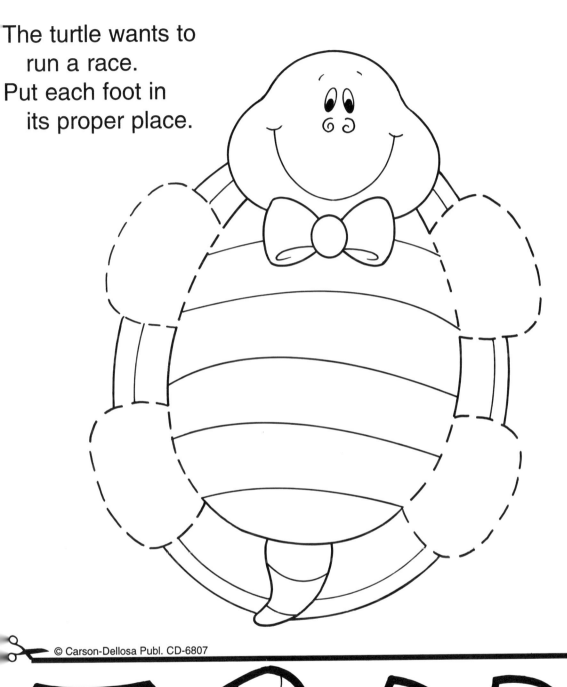

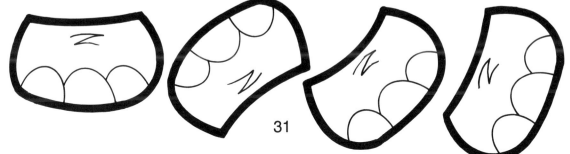

31

Cut out the pieces for Marty Mouse.
Paste them together to make him a house.

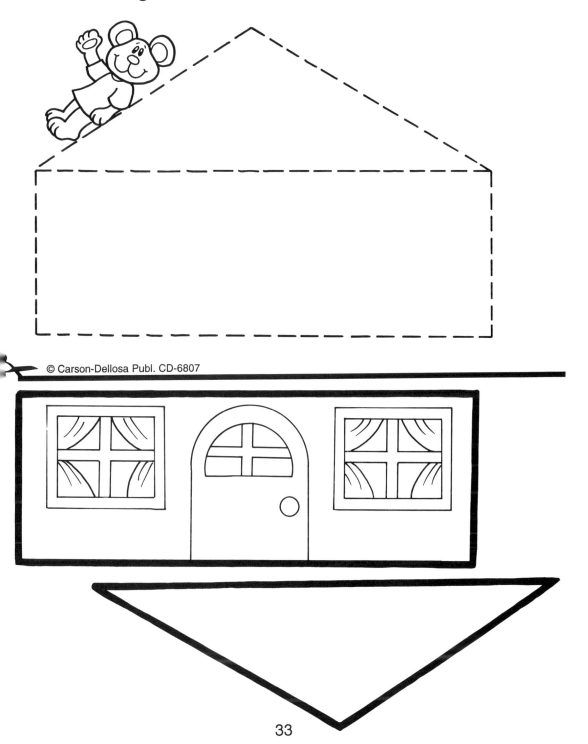

33

Cut out the shapes and paste them on.
This fish will smile from dusk until dawn.

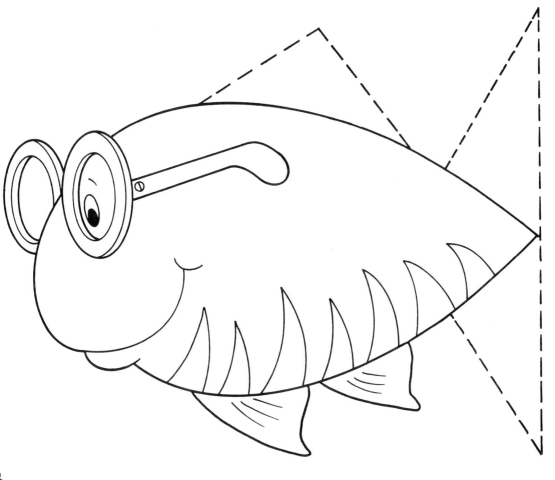

Decorate the flags for Jerry and Grace.
Cut them out on the thick lines and paste them in place.

37

When you get hungry, please do not scream!
Color, cut and paste a dish of ice cream.

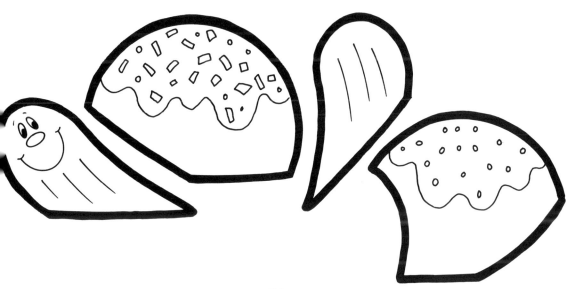

Binky juggles bright rubber balls.
He puts on a good show.
You can color, cut out and paste
Balls for him to throw.

This elephant's face is not complete.
Put her together so she can eat.

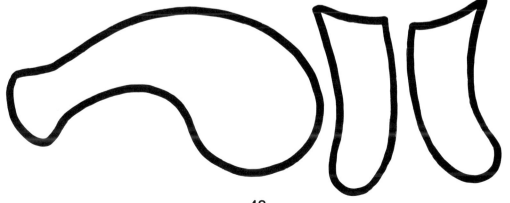

Won't you please help Jimmy and Stella?
It has started to rain and they need an umbrella.

Color and cut out the umbrella on the thick line. Paste it above Jimmy and Stella.

Nancy likes baseball and she has her own bat,
But to play on a team, she needs her own hat.

Color and cut out Nancy's hat on the thick line. Paste it on her head.

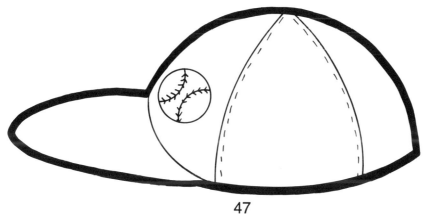

This alarm clock has lost its time.
Put it together so it can chime.

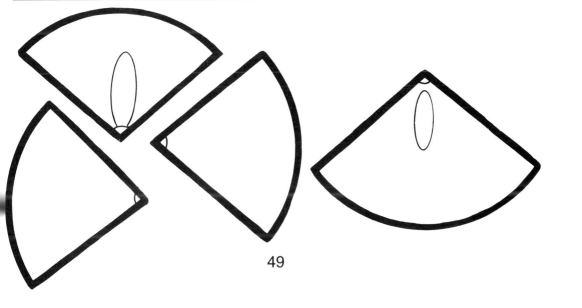

Would you like your own truck?

Then print your name on the side.

Fold on the line, jump in, and take a ride!

rint your name on the side of the truck. Color and cut it out on the
ick lines. Fold it on the dotted line. Your truck will stand up.

Humpty fell off the wall, and he's broken in two.
You can put him together – use your scissors and glue.
Color and cut out Humpty on the thick lines. Paste him on the dotted lines.

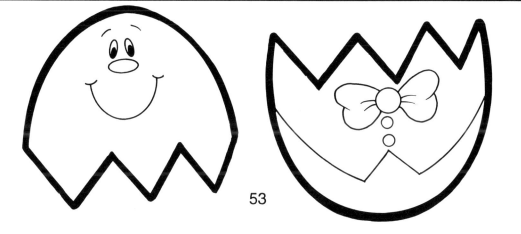

53

deep-sea diver, just look at him!
ut him together so he can swim.

As you look at these pieces,
Are you aware
That you can paste them together
To make a cute bear?

Color and cut out all of the
pieces on the thick lines.
Paste them together on
another sheet of paper to
make a bear.

Butterfly, butterfly, don't fly away!
Put her together so she will stay.

Cut on the thick lines. Paste the pieces to make a butterfly on another sheet of paper.

Kate Kangaroo is wearing a bonnet.
Put her together with her baby in her pocket.
Cut on the thick lines. Paste the pieces together on another sheet of
paper.

See how well you can cut all the lines below.

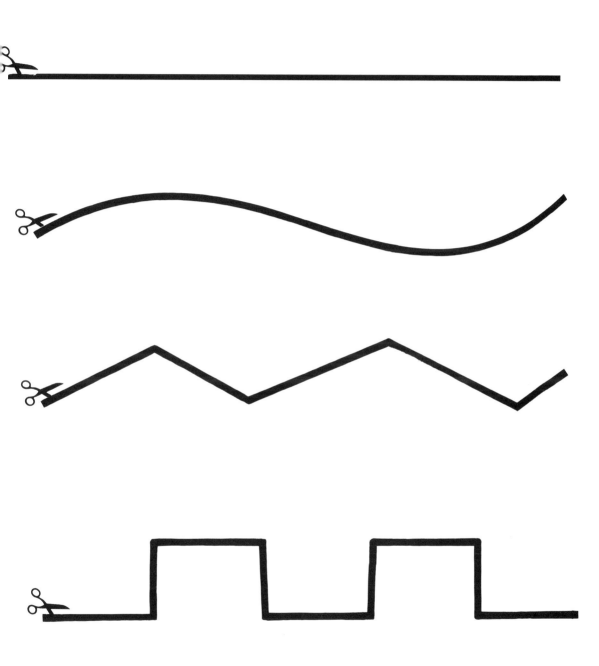